S0-AXJ-683

# FINGERSPELL

# FINGERSPELL

## Lindsay Illich

Black
Lawrence
Press

www.blacklawrence.com

Executive Editor: Diane Goettel
Book and Cover Design: Zoe Norvell
Cover Art: Hazel Meister

Copyright © Lindsay Illich 2020
ISBN: 978-1-62557-822-8

All rights reserved. Except for brief quotations in critical articles or reviews, no part of this book may be reproduced in any manner without prior written permission from the publisher: editors@blacklawrencepress.com

Published 2020 by Black Lawrence Press.
Printed in the United States.

In *Go Ahead In the Rain: Notes To A Tribe Called Quest*, Hanif Abdurraqib wrote, "There is plenty out there worth doing alone, but for everything else, there is a need for your people. It would behoove you to have a crew."

I dedicate this book to my crew—Hazel, Dobie, and Craig. I love you, always.

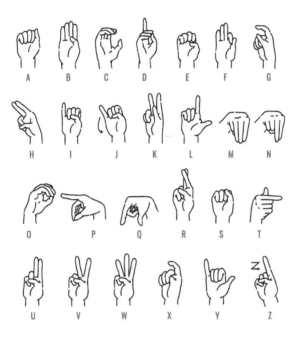

*finger·spell* - to spell out a word using the alphabet signs,
used when a word doesn't have a sign, for names, for emphasis,
or when the signer doesn't know the sign for a word.

# CONTENTS

# ARIEL

In the dream, instead of lady parts
down there, I had a Bundt cake—

slightly burned, dusted with confectioner's
sugar, but more obviously, its hole.

When I was young I was stupid.
I thought I was good for what I didn't

do. I've made a life of appearances.
You were *here*. I have the cave

left where we hollowed
out the pumpkin flesh,

our spoons clicking. And that was
some light. It, too, is a kind of

throat. The reason why people
make Bundt cakes is about increasing

surface area so that everybody
gets some crust. Design being the first

accommodation. Why does *obvious*
have to be a bad thing? The thing

is defined by absence. And you
aren't here.

# ARBORIST

Soon we were talking
thundercloud plums, blood-

good maples. In a copse
off the main road where they

kept mulch, a birch.
I showed you my plans,

the A2 of my daughter's atria,
asked if it was possible

to make the hydrangeas
blue. You said it's easy,

that I should bury
rusty nails or a sternal saw

near her, that the roots
would draw out the alkaline.

That it takes time but eventually
the acidity will change her.

# AUBADE

O morning earthsmell like small
bent basil, a child blinking open

wet with thanksgiving a
sky we lay under talking over

birdchatter we spoke the bee
tumble gradually an understanding our

lungs became pockets
handing out the days

saying here take it just take it
in your hand who knew you would

be so good at ax throwing what
aim I love the arc of arm

the fog of morning with my teeth
on your ear, the morning come

through the windows like children
awake now it's Christmas

all the lights your hand couldn't
we be opening each other

# A BIRD CLAIMS TO LIVE ONLY FOR THE SIMORGH

I worry. About magic. I say things and they
happen. A little house. A river and sailboats.

A boy. I said a blue and it came over me,
my body a beautiful nib, writing myself.

I loved arrogant birds and brick brunettes
full of roll presses, the beds of printers.

The hoopoe says don't brag about your love
because it's God that makes you prey,

it has nothing to do with you. Intricate
and strange are the ways love lights in us.

A young boy was rescued from the pond
at the end of our road yesterday. He had

fallen. The ice broke. Branches overhanging
the embankment. A neighbor saw through them

and went running into the water. The hoopoe
says it was God's eye that saw the boy's throat,

open and calling. I am devastated,
picturing my son in the water and quick

to take it back before someone

heard the thoughtshadow and thought it

a suggestion. I see rocks and think,
pockets. A high wall: brisk white shirts

flying down like heavy kites. Another
reason I'm terrified of writing fiction.

# BOILERPLATE

If you add a bell ringing
to any word you get a kind of love:

Earth-*ling*, star-*ling*, dar-*ling*.
Earthling, starling, darling—

with suckle, with succor, in situ,
as if love was the evidence of attention,

seedling to sapling. I love you wholly
with my mouth when I think

of words like Stockholm. Like Nebraska.
Like sycamore. To tell the truth

I've blown these words
in you, if only to register

their beauty against your brief
skin, words striking against

the tuning fork of your legs.
Just to hear their ringing.

# THE BOSTON CHILDREN'S HOSPITAL SABBATH ELEVATOR

Like spun glass, if you
pulled a strand

of his hair across
your lips, it would

draw blood. He asks
how needles

are made. The light
in the lobby is muted,

a glass wall
with water or

projections of water,
floors of aquatic life.

An elevator going
up and down,

stopping at every floor.
He said, but

no one's there.
When the doors

open.

# THE BRUTAL SCIENTIFIC

*Sturnella neglecta* for western meadowlark,
yellow throats. I also don't like

ironic t-shirts on children, the literal being
all they have. And in flight, a quiet

I didn't imagine was up here, like
I'm responsible for no one, the blithe

turbulence, a raised plastic glass, no
images but in things half remembered:

my god the clouds. We are water
pouring through letters, saturated

with meaning. So this is Chicago.

# CROSSING THE POTOMAC IN A SUPERSHUTTLE VAN

I saw Washington's Monument come into view
and another less recognizable domed one, the ladies

in the seat behind me going on about how warm
it is for February, and suddenly I feel childish

for being affected so at the sight of the city
which seemed now, after, archaic, the remains

of an idea. On the street, all manner of customary urbanity:
a congress of Asian men in suits and lanyards

announcing their official capacity, a bicycle
with white kicks spinning, a white man with a dark

beard in very tight pants with suspenders
crossing the street. A woman is wearing a sun

dress with bare legs, her hair loose and flowing
behind her. I had arrived wanting to feel American

but now I just miss my mother, waking up
in her house and hearing her going on about her business

vacuuming or emptying the dishwasher, which I took
as evidence of her loving me. At the hotel

I found the room, smaller than the pictures looked,

more vulnerable. I took a long shower and went to sleep

thinking about the portrait of Washington in the boat
crossing another river, its impossibilities like

how the ice doesn't freeze in shards like that
or how he wouldn't be able to keep his balance

with one leg up on the bow, especially during a storm.
Then it was light, well past morning, the sun falling

in a bright quadrilateral on the bed, and then from
the hall, the sound of someone vacuuming.

# THE DEAF AND AUSTERE GOSPEL

*for Angela Faye Smith, d. February 23, 1991*

First I prayed for my black heart
to be clean. Then
because aliens

meant anything could
happen, I prayed for E.T.
to die.

I prayed for the rapture
not to happen
because I loved the rims

of my body, what felt
like opening. Sometime
before all this

a man from my aunt's church
had me kneel on his
living room floor and

all the people there
laid hands on me
and I started praying

in a vowelish ocre
of real language, the vocative
whole of meaning.

And much later,

I prayed for you
to show yourself, as if

you were hiding. Then,
that you would be
found,

the night
shot through
with flashlight,

their single eyes scanning
the low brush, the sinking
of your body

like a stick I imagined
after. In Texas, small
manmade ponds

for livestock to drink from
are called stock tanks.
They keep animals

alive in periods
of drought. Now
I pray for

nothing. I don't want
anything, not eyes
to see or ears to hear.

# DESCRIPTION OF AN ABANDONED SILVER MINE

Full well, I knew: eyebrows from the couch,
a couplet of cinema. Remember on the train,

the men in orange robes, the clean cut
tonsure, the younger one reading on his tablet.

Wanting is terrible. I knew full well
standing at the kitchen sink.

Some directors have a way of expressing
musculature through light. Time is an optic.

From on high, pools of runoff, amber
on the shore, dark in the middle.

An immense and tragic beauty complete
with smelting piles and books we carried

loose in our arms like children.
You knew full well the water

piped in like music was boring.
It's stunning the depths we go to,

the carotid, conditions we negotiate
for an understanding: ores

and eithers, glittering among the coffee grounds,

in the elaborate filing and folding, towels

and trowels, vowels and vocatives, standing
at the mouth, wholesome and reckoning.

I want out and want in at the same time.

# EARLY JULY AND THE FAINT WHITE BUTTERFLIES

Fluttering and suspended, in accompaniment
with the air their delicate wings, and with each other,

what I remember of quickening, a kind of haunting
I felt before you were born, and then after,

in the bath, watching the twin plumes of milk
rise from my breasts to the water's surface,

how wasteful it felt to lie there, letting it happen,
yet how beautiful to watch the nourishment

of my body going into the world so materially,
as evidence of love, a flourishing like these

white lovelies scoring the air, their brief
and beautiful wingbeats like white hearts

and you running out to meet them, arms open.

# ECLIPSE

It wasn't our collective looking
up that united us (even if only gesturally)

nor was it the sharing (seconds, minutes,
the penumbra of the path of totality)

pictures of cracked pavement with light
through trees cast as shimmers

of bright crescents like signatures
of this exact moment when our moon

covered the star (along the dotted line,
almost completely aside from his errant

corona flaring), but perhaps it was
our asking how it was such a small

celestial body managed to overcome
such fury, even if only momentarily.

# EMPIRE

On sunblast days I sit outside, the white
undersides of my arms upturned

waiting. Because the sun, the sun also
sanitizes, and in my heart

I know myself to be a colonizer.
Remember the summer

we couldn't afford cable, watching
the same movie over and over, sweat

dripping off the window unit vent.
We were so innocent with our cigarettes,

weren't we. Beloved, this is just
to say that I don't think I would love

you if I knew you better. Let's love
each other like celebrities do, to a cavalcade

of shuttering, all the cameras on us.
The light is famous with wanting.

# FACES PASS BY, THEN

I wish you weren't dead because
I want to show you this

picture of a kitchen because
I can imagine you standing in it,

your arm wrapped around
an aluminum bowl, whisking with such

purpose. I've tried matching your
rhythm, or caught myself

trying to. Death hasn't stopped you
from arriving in my hand

holding a green measuring
cup, or in my ear, a flutter

of gold leather earrings
the shape of leaves.

Or at an intersection, waiting
to turn left, watching the stream

of faces pass by, then
some eyes meet mine

and I think for a beat
it's you.

# FAULT LINES

The first word I thought of
when I heard the diagnosis was

*retarded,* and I was ashamed.
Followed by the crotch-buttoned

black teddy, how I took it.
I thought she would never even

miss it. Hours of gray ash
on the concrete floor like gray

snow. Or the time I walked
right past her in the lobby

and pretended she was
a light fixture. I didn't pick up.

After fifty-seven calls
I didn't pick up.

The summer we got fleas
in the house, the constant

vacuuming, the gross
everywhere of itching. The egg,

double-yolked, that meant
someone would die

and I knew who. It was
when we were in the desert,

a silence, the emptiness
I deserved. Then it was ants,

not knowing I was on them,
the meringue welts.

Or when I wasn't:
in front of the camera,

your cool eye. And Texas,
acoustic for its vast I'm never

there for you. I loved
the quiet of no one,

the upside
down of mother.

Like I said, all I wanted
was to find a comfortable

pair of pajamas. I wanted
the looseness of being,

the tethers of drawstrings.
Around me. I wanted plaid.

I wanted thin,
breathable flannel.

# FEVER

That night the fever returned,
her forehead a hotplate,

her hand a flame. The bed
wasn't big enough

for our trouble. We passed
her back and forth

when the spot where she lay
grew hot, the hours slow

and she was the clock,
her legs kicking

for what shore I don't know.
I don't think she did

either.

# FINGERSPELL

The sign for shoes,
not a fingerspell.

I hear a plane,
my hand takes off,
obliquely.

The shore, attached
to the water.

Tall trees beyond
the road, their roots
beyond my elbow.

I sign spring.
When no one is looking,
clouds. The rain

deciding who. Cells,
alone with silence
and books of time,

stacked beside
gestures of opening
books. The city beyond

walking up staircases,
inside a room where
no one is sitting.

It's evening. We
take off our shoes.
I show you a video

of murmuring starlings
and wonder where
they learned to say

the world that way,
what same night darkness
was giving way inside them.

# FLIGHT TRACKER

I no longer consider crashes
a possibility, despite what I see
beyond the glass: yellow lights

flashing, the slight metallic
surface of a wet runway, like
an invitation. Rows of planes,

each window on the fuselage a face
on a birch bough. I sit attuned
to flight, anticipate the letting down

of landing gear. In these hours
when you are nowhere on earth
I do consider the possibility.

At night, the airport is hollowed out
like a brain that took blow after blow.
This waiting is a splint

my body's wrapped against.
This waiting keeps me upright.
It means things are still up in the air:

your plane, our sadnesses, your brutal
diagnosis. All that's left is the all clear
you need before descent. My phone says

you're on the ground. Then, I see it
approaching the gate, the single
arm of the jetway stretched out

to receive you.

# GENIUS

Like good genes I thought
You either had it or didn't

I would obsess over author
Bios in the back matter

Specifically birth year compared
To my own thinking I was

Falling behind oh honey there's
Room I think you come into it

Suddenly like light, let there, or
Money, or a devastating blow from

Out of nowhere yes, it's called
A stroke for a reason

# GIRL (ACT I)

I found places
Where I could go

Without a shirt
And barefoot, a hot

Pavement I saw
Cars pass but I was

The one going places
See the bunk bed,

See the sharp-faced
Faucet, show me

A girl with a wet
Face then one day

I thought my eyebrows,
They're weird

And took a razor
To one which was

The first act ending

# GLASS SELF, OR DRIVING HOME FROM BASEBALL PRACTICE

A sky cut through with a streak
Of white, the cyan afternoon

Pronouncing your leaving
In a contrail (of course not your

Actual flight, that happened
Years ago). Mornings, listing

Through rooms, in extopian
Deluge. Rains of coffee,

Then a sudden snow,
Forsaken forsythia, magnolia—

What we take as the signs
Of new are lost, a green

Without bloom. This is no more
A tragedy than it was losing

You. The trick is to stay
Conducive. At night I wrap

My arms in copper, sit
In a bath and stare at plugs.

The window. I consider how
The glass was sand, blown

With fire. First a heat,
Then burn, then the clarity

Of being seen through.

# GOLDLIGHT

I wouldn't recommend having kids
as a treatment for depression.

Just take the morning large as a room
and bright as eggs, plain

as sweet'n low on cornflakes,
love poured over. Or summer,

the swimming pool with
all the chairs pointing toward

her. What is the world
for tedium, the feathers

around your eyes, for
goldlight and alive can

I swallow it, the sun,
an ocean of worry sitting

in my throat, waiting.

# HATCHLING

In the morning a thought
like a blue thread

from your satin bomber:
your wrist. Wrist. The sky, alone.

The ribbons inside me
are the ribbons inside you.

The egg pulls air from outside
the shell, the animal heart

beating without being
tethered to a body, without

our strange umbilicus. Until.
A small tap. Then another.

Then a beak, a breath,
then a breaking open

into this broken world.

# HUNGER

The truth is that I know,
that is to say, I count it

among things I count as true
in a world of mutability:

seven almonds equals
one Weight Watcher's point.

This sadness is everywhere,
the calculus of lips, as if

accumulation were not subject
to joy, as if one shouldn't.

Grow. I want. More
than three grapes.

I need a caloric identity
beyond its singular

animalness, as if
I were eating for the

whole world.

# I ELABORATE MY STATUS AS A COLONIZER

Our orbital bodies, cast across the water
into deep and vast, corroborated,

asking what's wrong. June and August,
the dog light, piles of I hardly know you.

Love this mutability, our calving away
from we were never really together

were we. In the morning, in the mirror,
on the phone where we were living.

If only we could grow young together,
come retrospectively so we could see

what good we were all at once,
walk through the gallery of weren't

we beautiful, and look at that one:
they had no idea what they were doing,

and then the yesterday, plainly
like invasion, you were mine.

# I EXPLAIN THE DARK CENTER

It started with your eyes
calling from the tub to *come*

*get me,* bring your warm
sorrow. The part of losing you

I can't get over is how you grow
despite my not watering:

I threw seeds out the window
and this year I pick all the tomatoes

I want. You said, it's the humidity.
Yes, I approve the antediluvian.

No rain but everywhere lush
the Earth found blue.

Your hip crests, a caldera of pumice
we rubbed and rubbed like worry

until we were worn down
to the bone.

# INSTRUCTIONS FOR SURVIVAL

I thought my son might be a poet
When he asked, barely three years old,
*So this is it? Every day's the same?*

Son, hold the sun against your chest
Long enough and love grows
Like bacteria and millions of years later

You'll climb out of bed onto land
And breathe your first like a volcano
Erupting and then a girl

Is reading the book and comes
Suddenly alive. We are born.
Because we survive by determining

the wonder out of gray ore.
We survive spore like, hovering
along coasts, pointing out species

of trees. We survive by noticing
at closing when they cut the lights
at Target, a soft blue replaces the white

fluorescence. We moved through
the light as if buoyed by it. There
are nouns all around us and more

to come and that
is the kind of joy I'm betting on.

# JAW

A woman, I don't even know
how she's related to me but I heard

she was a waitress at a place called—
this is embarrassing—

anyway, she worked there
even after she got old and

then this one Saturday night
something awful happened.

There's no other way to say it but
*prolapse.* Her uterus detached.

Whenever I'm in a new relationship
I ask the guy if he's ever heard of it,

as a test. The only one who had
said it happened to some of their cows.

*Hotdogs down a hallway*, he said.
Anyway, all I could think of was all the work

she did. Of the finishing and pushing
and her children and then the mess.

Of stuff hanging out down there.
And after she was dead was when

we found out about this happening.
She wrote about it in a letter to her sister,

And made a joke about the whole
thing. She wrote, *I slipped on a pickle*

*and my womb fell out!* I thought
a long time about that exclamation point.

# KANSAS

Sunset on the night the storm was coming,
the sky had the look of an enormous crescendo,

the highway a measure whose notes are held far,
far down the road. We head into the night

uncharacteristically upbeat. At one point
we even pull over for a bag of tacos.

I held the baby's hand from Salina to Wichita.
At points along the fences, colorful makeshift

crosses. The stations were mostly ballet folklorica,
preachers who worried about personal debt,

and one we stayed on for awhile was interviewing
the head coach of the Kansas City Chiefs. The night,

far off in the distance, looked slate, darker
at the horizon. We keep going toward it,

no sense in worrying at this point about
the car stalling, or the fact that none of us

has gloves, the baby completely out of milk.
It feels like I can see clear to the next county, then

a berm of trees, left alone to concern myself
with the book in my lap, knowing

I don't have much light left to read by.

# LAJITAS

At the live
edge

of this
animal,

I lose
the historical

to the octopus
self: cups

of wanting,
like West

Texas. The
mesa

rise
across string,

your arm
running through

a state
of breath

and cottonwood.

# LARKSPUR

Searching for where to buy the small
Japanese facial razors

I thought, larkspur that's a thing,
right, or tiger lilies, which is July:

oh we lie brilliantly awake, our soft
bodies slant, pinging back

and forth are you asleep yet
are you asleep, putting my phone

down and picking it back up again,
checking on what I'm not sure

# THE LIE

Like a murdered body might, it was stuffed
in a white trash bag then stuffed
in the trunk of a 97 Honda Accord.

I bought it on layaway, for $337 plus
a finance charge, but it was over
before I finished paying for it.

A year passed. It was in there in April,
During the glut of lovebugs, intersections
turned swarms of copulation.

It was in there, silent, during hurricane season,
the maps of suns coming at us, the gulf
like a catcher's mitt.

It was there when I spotted
a bolt of tulle in a ditch and thought of you.
The car was acting strange and reckless.

What I like best about the new car
is how innocent it is, its emptiness.
I can drive around without having to

think about everything, like I got away
with something. Until the dealership called.
They said I'd left some personal items

in the trunk of the trade in, did I
want to come by and pick them up.
I said, *No, that's ok.* Then the guy said,

*But there's a wedding dress in there,*
and I said, *Oh—that's not mine.*
*I don't care what you do with it.*

# MAMA EXPLAINS THE EXTERIORITY OF INVENTION (THE TALK)

1.

When she told me what the body becomes
in the hands of another body,

I saw the sea in chevrons, a crowded
din, the mechanics of desire,

among them a diagram of a lightbulb,
the filament pulsing in it and lo,

a new idea graphically rendered
in a way I understood how to articulate.

2.

When I read quote *the good Yvonne*
*and bad Yvonne, two of the four times*

*I've been in love* unquote, I understood
genealogy like eyes, they have the same, or gait,

I am yours. Knew I was yours
because of our gray flecked dark

narrative style. Do our mothers bear
us or do we bear their resemblance?

3.

When I don't recognize anyone
in a paragraph, I check

the metal key above the chimney
to see if the flue is open,

for why else wouldn't I feel
your draft, my desire

a fluency with open,
the fingers of thinking.

4.

Walking in the city, making libraries
of my thighs (I'm always lending),

books flying in and out of them
like birds, a murder of pages, the murmur

become quarto the quarto become
codex and we are endlessly

scrolling.

# MILK CAVE

The light long into the street,
the dark tepid dark, the wash

wilderness of teeth
against, sedan down pavement.

All the low tinning and
overhead a jet.

I live far from it.
The glass pitcher of dead

peonies I watch timbers
of light fall

across her face, her
mouth pulling deeply

at my nipple, which,
what is it there for

save her succor, save
the blaze mouth

who tenders me, save
the stark raving quiet,

the sit here and thinking.

# MORNING WHITE LIKE FORGIVENESS

In the morning white like forgiveness
the snow drenched branches buckled

like broken wrists and one eye squint
just waking, I'm glad you took

that picture of me sitting up in bed
especially because the central figure

is my left nipple. I love it! I love its
young small tautness! The sunlight

and all the vanishing points
are possible. Noon is possible.

Thaw and thanksgiving, possible.
I love how it covers everything.

# MOTHER

If I could go to her I would show her
a picture of my daughter sleeping,

let her listen to the spring night
greening, show her the webpage

with little white flags on all the cities
where I've landed since I signed

into Google. I would walk her
to the kitchen and show her

the mango wood salad tongs
and the air plants embedded

in crystals that her sister mailed her
on her birthday. I would show her

my belly so she would get naked more,
sit around and bask in the flat

goodness of what nineteen
looks like in panties. What was it

I was so sad about, I would ask
her. I would have hated me,

appearing out of nowhere
with answers, just like a mother.

# THE NOURISHMENT OF MY BODY

It was the lightning first, after dark,
that made me realize it was dark,

your figure against the window,
the quatrefoil and ikat, the blank

face you get when I ask a question
you don't want to hear. I cleaned

until I was tired of cleaning. I cleaned
until I loved the house more than

the children. I found dried spots
of breast milk on the hardwood

from had to be months ago. What a pity
any of it was wasted this way. Like

afternoon wasn't enough, then evening,
low dark clouds ferrying past lighter,

their ineluctable shearing
against each other.

# ON ADDRESSIVITY (WHAT'S WRONG? WHAT'S WRONG? WHAT'S WRONG?)

I'm a body of organs I don't recognize
I mean its notes, these words I thought

there would be a morning you would look
at me and say something about what's

wrong, about what you're thinking because
we tend to experience sequentiality

as a substitute for substantivity
as if life were ambulation no two

ways about it like those visitation
booths in prisons I imagine everything

they say is underscored by saying it
into the heavy receiver the cradle all

that attention focused on the mouth
then one of us is finished talking

and the other takes his turn and
so on

# PITTSBURGH OR BUDAPEST

When I woke up this afternoon
it was raining, and for a second I thought

it was morning, like I had lost the day.
You said they found diamonds. Not to

worry about money anymore. Later
in the produce aisle, velvet peaches,

cut flowers in the distance, like I don't
deserve you. At night on tv (always the tv)

recusal like doors blowing shut,
raindrops like asterisks, excepting.

The stone fruit of your knee caps.
I want us to be a Pittsburgh or Budapest,

a city where rivers meet, rivers
because we are the bodies

in their beds, current lathing
between our legs. I can't help

but think of you as
the rain, as *en route*.

# PLAY

The first boy
drove a grain truck
and dry humped me
on the carpet somewhat
respectfully, kind of
like the next one who
made me initiate
then held my head
down, like I was
underwater. Later
he told me he loved
me and that I had
the biggest clit he'd
ever seen. I loved
Dr. Pepper and doing
my bangs with an old
curling iron crusted
with hairspray. It made
it easier to hold clean
hair, especially fine
hair that usually fell
off the rod before
you could get any
height. I learned
that teasing helped.
There was another boy
who did everything to me
a person can do to another
person (or so I thought
at the time) and then

he left. Then another (I'm tired
of verbs). Then another.
Until I was a mother,
And there weren't any
Others. House. Dead.
It was a relief
to be done playing.

# PLINIAN

Here and now
makes nowhere,

dark and brief. It's
Maine. There

are so many clothes
before the bare

heart of you.

# A PROBLEM OF TRANSCRIPTION FOR DISCOURSE ANALYSIS

Brother, I can't find a word
that expresses brackets in speech.

*Parenthetically*
but more.

I'm tempted to say
brackets are purely textual

[I miss you]

and therefore useless
in synchronous communication

All I'm asking you to consider
are that the conditions

that gave rise to the need for brackets
are predicated on

asynchronicity [which is your
not being here].

Think about my hands
as gestures, a means

of holding
what should be said.

# PROOF

Maybe the reason I think
I'm going to die soon is that
I'm going to die soon. My father

refuses to get on an airplane.
This condition is chronic.
Something called

*wedding ring dermatitis*
when a person after years
of wearing one suddenly develops

an allergy to nickel. That's
commitment. My mother
ironed her hair. Some mornings

I look at my tongue, scalloped
at the edges where it rests
against my teeth. A mouth

is a harbor. I keep myself
from saying it means
I'm worthless to him. I crack

open the window and let
my room fill with cold, the chill
come alive. My breath. I see you.

# PUSH PLAY AND RECORD

I made a tape of myself
trying to speak in tongues

(*push play and record
at the same time*, you said).

The tape deck's clear
plastic lid had come off

somewhere, so I could press
play and touch the capstans turning,

feel their thinking like eyes
in the machine. And when they said

I had pinworms you said,
*don't wear panties under your gown*

*tonight*. And when you came in
to say goodnight, you brought

a flashlight. You switched it on
and said, *I'm gonna put this*

*under the covers*. You said,
*Don't worry, they'll go to the light.*

# A QUESTION I WANT TO ANSWER YES

First, the small doable:
eggs, a pan of lasagna. Maybe

a fern is a way of thinking,
a fiddlehead explaining herself.

Perhaps the morning,
a sharp book out of soil

and seed, pages for leaves.
Through the window,

I smell her fullness, her life
a question I want to answer yes

and the table is a list where words
get to know each other,

where I want cohesion, a sense
we're making it, going together

like white shirts with everything,
which is deliberate. So now

the imperative mood:
survey her walking, one bone

next to the next like perfect
sentences, the known and new

driving down like a blade
into the fields of your body.

# RAPTURE AS EPIPHANY

Pilgrim, after love we despair
of knowledge beyond our nudities.

We love, then comes gnosis.
Skin then marrow,

a broad summer of light
rays, each leaf an eachother

of treeform. You'll see the sun-
dered fragments of sculpture

in the clouds and understand
how the universe fits together.

Or, downtown, the vertical glass
looking down on you

will release in your heart
an idea: all the windows

hewn for the moment you
looked up. The breeze swirls

as a car passes the intersection,
momentarily lifting street

stuff, our hypothetical pockets
emptied as we are caught up.

# RATIOS GOLDEN OR OTHERWISE

The ideal of symmetry is confirmed in the body:
look at my arms, always matching

or lungs or temples or eyes or any organ
in twos: these breasts are heavy

with suggestion, full of confirmation
bias: I might be the most imperfect vehicle

for reasoning even though I know bold
is the body who bases her assumptions

on ratios golden or otherwise:
Love, I've lost the ability

to navigate a winter from a hallway
a summer from a road

I thought we were the same
above ground as below, the root

system a mirror symmetry of our
branch sway, the Blackland Prairie

a dark galaxy, salt for stars:
I thought my capacity for sadness

demonstrated a proportionate positive
like if I felt this way you would match

it, lobe for lobe, even though
the principle of symmetry is evidenced

in the physical not the emotive world:
here, precarity, then a cleaving into water,

a sadness the size of Connecticut.

# THE SHAPE OF GOD

We drive into the city looking for a place that makes
homemade tortillas, the coastline interrupted
with our questions: who is the diarist and what
do the colors on the watertower mean?

I wasn't listening when I was pretending to.
We drove into the big tunnel laying tracks
for lunch. I hope they have enchiladas,
one said, pretending not to listen to us.

Another said he misses his dad. He had
this weird thing where he always had dead
skin hanging off his lip, like half-shed snake
skin. I kiss him squarely on it. Freud said

the oceanic feeling we have inside that makes
us long for the infinite is the ghost of womb life:
all our dreams are amniotic. The Tex-pat
bartender made me a prickly-pear margarita

and brought us plates of beans and rice.
December and industry and the cacao winnowing
machine and on strands of my hair the dust collects
so when you sweep you get these disgusting

galaxies of detritide and time, the car
emerging from the tunnel and flying toward
the Best Buy where my eight year old
is picking out his first laptop, the handmade

marshmallow's from Lydia's bakery in Revere
waiting in the trunk. I look back and think how awful
the traffic looks. The hole in my daughter's

heart isn't God-shaped because it's getting
smaller. And that isn't how these things work.

# SNOW

I don't know
if this is old or new

grief but
maybe it grows

by accumulation so
old or new

it is the same
drift, each

flake falling
an addendum

and there goes
the porch, the felled

tree stump, window-
sill then fenceline

it's all the same snow
old or new the snow

into which
the heart sinks

# SPECTRUM

Tonight, I'm the loneliest I've ever been.
It's been a week since our conversation

(if you can call it that) about snow.
How it must be cleared quickly no matter

how we feel about going out. Today,
I saw myself in screens, reflected in their

dark glass. Spectral, like an idea
when really I wanted to be bloody.

They told me to write you without
emotion. They said, tell him explicitly

what you need. What came out:
Concentrate all your energy

at the rims of our openings.
Paragraphs, like marriages, begin

in certainty and end in spectacle:
Part metal, part bird. I open and close

your mouth like my hand was inside you.
Tuesday I gave you the letter. I hear

our daughter waking up. She calls
out for me, and I get her. In the morning,

the light went through the house, lit every
surface, like the house was an ear

tilted toward the dawn, like it
was trying hard to listen.

# TAMPA MIDWINTER

Floating up from the pool patio
two women's voices

singing a stripped down
version of "I Wanna Dance

With Somebody" which
tonight seems to ring

truer than Whitney's.
It was very sad and the amp

was turned up too loudly
for such a small party

and the bay, just sitting there,
like an enormous dark

indifference.

# THESIS STATEMENT

Some say a thesis is the point.
Some say a thesis is what you arrive at.
Some say a thesis is a claim with reasons.
Some say a thesis is the single unifying
idea about which the entire work is focused.
Some say a thesis should be written
first. Some say a thesis, if the issue is
controversial, should be delayed
until all the evidence is laid out.
Some say without a thesis
you're incoherent. Some say a thesis
artificially expresses a supposition
about relevance and accuracy
you only partially affirm but make
necessarily because the features
of the genre make such a supposition
not only appropriate but expected.
All day the thesis is stating, upright
in his righteousness, pointing forward,
following his own slick schtick.

# THIS IS LATE CAPITALISM

The flight was fourteen and a half hours,
not even close to the farthest I've been

away from you. What if being human
means being unrequited, the opposite

of fruit. We cultivate a kind of
unhome, which is why we look at fire,

why we write headlines in the form
of questions to which the answer is always

no. I like to think of love as a city,
all the elevators full of people waiting

for their floors, avenues and arteries,
the commuting of sentences, which is why

it's hard for me to look at you, why
envelopes, torn open, ask for it.

This is late capitalism! We are dying
for more coffee! The affording!

The evening and the night, the plums
overripe, the juniper and basil, I miss

your blazes, the telemetry of your face,
oh the fuselage of you, humming.

# TUESDAY

I put down the baby knowing
I can't ever put down the baby.

Children are relentless, like
consciousness, her eyes the room

I walk into and forget what I'm doing
there. I'm picking up the baby,

a wolf, howling and writhing,
alive with wake: I'm being ground

into bone meal and burned, ash for eyes.
The moon. I wish I could swallow it

and die and be done with
the guilt of having something more

I want to be doing
rather than. Because she can,

because she wants to,
because that's what babies do

while I'm not the Tuesday
I imagined I would be.

# UNCOVERED

Darkness takes separate things
and makes them indivisible.

The sky and horizon, body against
body, the smell of earth dredged,

the blade dug in, turning up
what was hidden. You've uncovered

me, our nudities grounding us
in the actual, our bodies' inevitable

darkness: I understand you.

# UNPERCHED

I stood, Aristotelian, stretched out
my arms and wrote *nectar*.

My arms were limbs of trees,
birds among them.

At desks the children, metal
leveling feet on linoleum.

The large windows like eyes,
hummingbirds flying out

my mouth, flying up,
looking for a way out.

# VIEW FROM THE SHOWER WINDOW OVERLOOKING THE BACKYARD

You were holding me.
You were holding me

on your hip in the shower
and warm the light and soft

the steam on the glass
and steady

the sound of water hitting
the plastic curtain:

I was certain. I was afforded
a view. Our skin was radiant.

My hair was clinging to the side
of my face. I was enormous.

I was enormous and you
were the arms holding me up.

# WAITING TO BOARD MY SPIRIT "HOME OF THE BARE FARE" FLIGHT

Eating "Sinfully Thin Kale and Pomegranate
Popcorn," I get a text from Mom

saying that the pregnancy test
following your second round of IVF

came back negative. From the plate
glass windows tiny motes of snow

barely perceptible, more easily so
if foregrounded against an object of color:

a hunter green corrugated dumpster,
a dark blue American Airlines trailer

like an old-fashioned hotel's
message system, empty boxes

waiting to be filled. Even the yellow
fuselage appears ready to carry me

safely to the next world, or really
just Tampa. But the snow. The snow

scattering everywhere, her dust
evidence of a beauty beyond

being of use, for carrying or
delivering us from anything.

# WAKING WHEN WEATHER IS HAPPENING

In the dark
full quiet
I recognize the snow

And imagine it
settling on the new
shoots of daffodil

I hear you reach
For your phone
Its glow on the ceiling

What a beautiful
Interference

# WHAT SHE WAS LOOKING FOR

It was hot. You were bare-
legged. The sheets were old

and soft. The space was masculine
with neutrals, like furniture become

timid in her presence. Ask her
what she was looking for

in your mouth. Ask her
what's with the beets

that time she called you over
to rub the juice on your lips.

That summer we put in
a garbage disposal and it wasn't long

until cherry tomato vines
came up and took over the fence

and she said she has to burn it
and came back with a can of gasoline.

When you tell her the paint
won't come off your legs,

she says, *Hold still. This should
take that off*, and you were elastic

and heady with the smell, ocean-
soaked, fluid, burning the back

of your throat. A voice
in your head saying, *Drink.*

# THE WOMAN WHO RODE THROUGH A TORNADO IN A BATHTUB AND LIVED

The night she sailed
her body felt light as an A4 page,

the inert become vehicle, and look—
the house, like a pancake in a black skillet,

the outer bank a smooth white beach
she sails past like it was a margin she blew out

as easily as a birthday candle, then
morning, the cut lemon on the counter, squeezed,

its middle seam lying open like the baby's
legs, getting diapered, thinking

I'm not like that. She wasn't airborne
for more than a minute, but it lasted

all night, tall without malevolence.
She thought it was bedbugs but that was just

New Jersey. She saw everything she wasn't
saying on people's yards like debris.

Her therapist said the tornado was a symptom
of her loneliness, that it was an attempt

to reckon with her reactive isolation.

This insults the page flying through the night.

The page says, *I want you to fuck me.*
The page, easy white inchoate,

doesn't pretend to cohere with anything
(doesn't it?), yet the aerial, the dramatic

fencing from here: look how far you can see.

# WORK EMAILS

Decision comes through the body:
we may not say this is how we

want to live but this is how
we're doing it. Above us on a bridge,

regular people pass with umbrellas,
sensible shoes, a plan

while we lack vocabulary
for preparedness. For some time

the week has been the smallest
unit of our being, whereas

it used to be a day. Time
in birdseye, taking in

a continent like that astronaut
on Twitter. I want to be

an ocean against your coast.
I could be so me out at sea,

thinking what on earth
do people do all day

and who is that man
sitting next to me

talking about work.

# X-RAY

Itsy bitsy
back board

against your
itsy bitsy back,

me in a lead
apron. Outside,

ice coming down
like salt.

I feel it bounce
like the radiation

blowing through
your small bones.

It was all I could do
to keep from

jumping behind
the curtain

and screaming
at the technician,

*I have a right
to see.*

# YOUR HAPPENING

I promise to work on my handwriting,
to keep the truth in it, remember

like yr hand sliding under
the cup of my bathing suit top,

our bodies newly beached, the water
how it skimmed over us, reading everything

we were, and slender the fluke
of your happening in me. I promise

it won't be like this forever because
I would be insufferable, saying

crazy shit like *ink drawing nigh*
*the margin*, like I think

people actually talk like that.

# ZENITH

You could tell I'd been drinking
from the way I tasted, my body

a reverse front range, recognizable
for miles, like the Mariana trench.

I was a calendar I wanted to fill
with your appointments,

your chest a bank of windows, strands
of saffron in the glass tube

of your torso, August over:
there was a child. God bless

those machines I read
easier than her face

and the early morning, when nothing
is on, I hear her soft breathing,

see her nose in silhouette,
the light from the window growing

lighter, the grass beyond,
the Gulf wind, the fronds of our

mimosa, her pink listing
and this life I was after

having somehow arrived.

# NOTES

"A Bird Claims to Live Only For the Simorgh" borrows its title from a section heading of Farid ud-Din Attar's "The Conference of Birds" (approximately line 2824)

"The Lie" was written after James Galvin's poem, "The Sadness of Wedding Dresses" that appeared in the Best American Poetry 2015 anthology.

"On Addressivity": Bakhtin used this term to describe how discourse shapes its answer in how the speaker/writer addresses the audience/reader: "The word in living conversation is directly, blatantly, oriented toward a future answer-word."

"What She Was Looking For" - After Ocean Vuong's "Someday I'll Love Ocean Vuong," and Roger Reeves's "Someday I'll Love Roger Reeves," which was after Frank O'Hara's "Katy."

"The Woman Who Rode Through a Tornado in a Bathtub and Lived" was based on a story from the Washington Post on January 24, 2017 about a 75 year old woman who did indeed survive a tornado having ridden it out in her bathtub, in the air.

# ACKNOWLEDGMENTS

Many thanks to the editors of publications where some of these poems first appeared: *Burnside Review, Columbia Journal, Cordite Poetry Review, Crab Orchard Review, Foundry, New Madrid, The Mantle, Nimrod International Journal of Prose and Poetry, Jet Fuel Review, Passages North,* and *Virga: A Journal of Poetry.*

Also, I'm thankful to those who made this work better along the way: Diane Goettel at Black Lawrence Press; my first readers, Melissa Anyiwo, Pebble Brooks, Heather Falconer, Don Gervich, David Miller, Rebecca Paynich, Kara Provost, Sarah Shane, and Patricia Stephens; Emily Davidson and Angela Lombardo at the Boston Children's Hospital Down Syndrome Clinic; Rachel Coleman, the host and creator of the show *Signing Times;* Melissa Smith, my co-author of *Teach Living Poets;* Danielle Legros Georges for choosing "Eclipse" for the Mayor of Boston's Poetry Program; Kirsten Miles at Tupelo Press and the poets from the first Tupelo Press 30/30 Project; Gregory Pardlo and Natalie Diaz whose insights as workshop leaders at the Fine Arts Work Center came at a critical time in the writing of this book; Nancy Young and Allison Bayer for generously opening their home in Provincetown; Rachel Zucker for producing the podcast *Commonplace: Conversations With Poets (And Other People)*; my professors and classmates at Texas A&M University; social media friends; and finally, to all of the writers and artists too numerous to name whose work nourishes my creative spirit, the evidence of which is apparent in these pages.

Thanks, also, to my academic institution, Curry College, for granting me a sabbatical to support this work, for providing institutional funding to attend AWP and several Fine Arts Work Center poetry workshops, and for giving me the opportunity to teach creative writing classes.

And to you. Thank you.

**Lindsay Illich** is the author of *Rile & Heave* (Texas Review Press, 2017) and the chapbook *Heteroglossia* (Anchor & Plume, 2016). *Rile & Heave* won the Texas Review Press Breakthrough Prize in Poetry. She teaches at Curry College in Milton, Massachusetts.